The Natural World
COLORING BOOK

LIBRO PARA COLOREAR DE
El mundo natural

por/by: Dr. Joshua Lawrence Patel Deutsch
illustrator: Afzal Khan

Sun
Sol
Mercury
Mercurio
Venus
Venus
Earth
La Tierra
Mars
Marte
Jupiter
Júpiter
Saturn
Saturno
Uranus
Urano
Neptune
Neptuno

Other books by this author

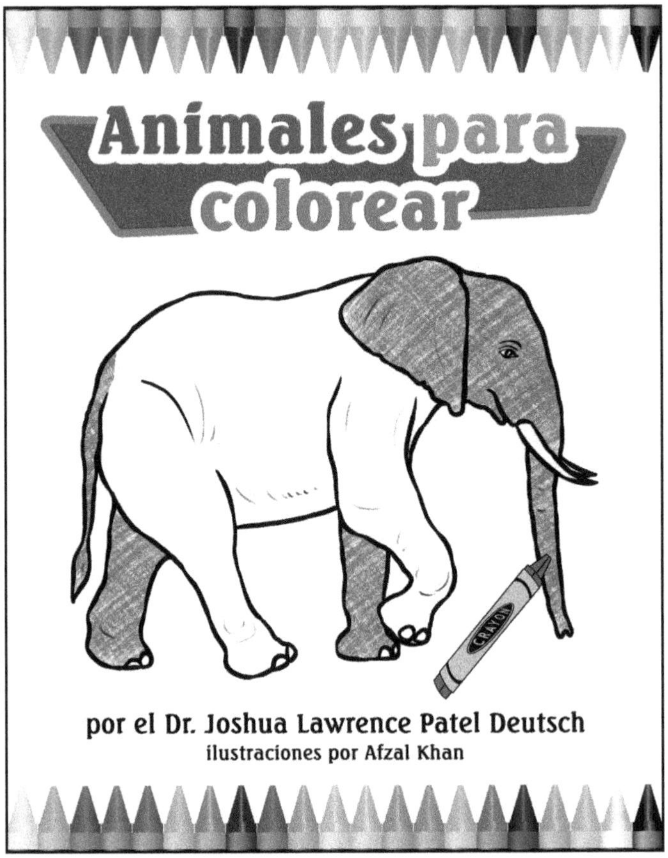

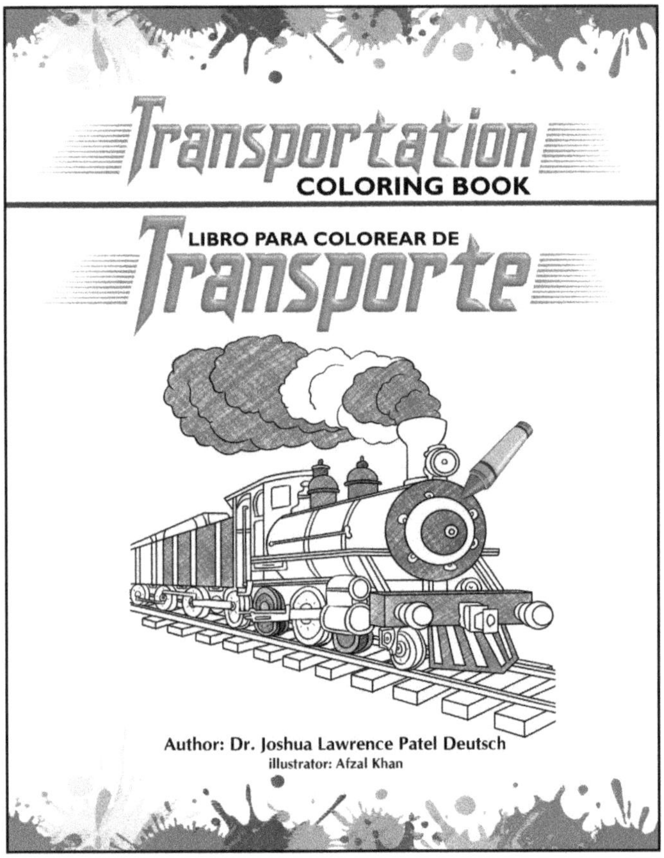